WHY WAR

IS NEVER

A GOOD

IDEA

Alice Walker

Illustrations by **Stefano Vitale**

HarperCollins*Publishers*

WHY WAR

IS NEVER

A GOOD

IDEA

Though War speaks
Every language
It never knows
What to say
To frogs.

Picture frogs
Beside a pond
Holding their annual
Pre-rainy-season
Convention.

They do not see War
Huge tires
Of a
Camouflaged
Vehicle
About to
Squash
Them flat.

Though War has a mind of its own
War never knows
Who
It is going
To hit.

Picture a donkey
Peacefully
Sniffing a pile
Of straw
A small boy
Holds
The end
Of its
Frayed
Rope
Bridle.

They do not see it
They are both thinking
Of dinner
The boy
Is hoping for
Polenta & eggs
Maybe a carrot
Or apple
For
Dessert.

Just above
Them
Something dark
Big as
A car
Is
Dropping.

Though War has eyes
Of its own
& can see oil
&
Gas
& mahogany trees
& every shining thing
Under
The earth

When it comes
To nursing
Mothers
It is blind;
Milk, especially
Human,
It cannot
See.

Picture a woman
Beside a window
She is blissful
Singing
A lullaby
A baby twirls
A lock of her
Dark hair
Suckles
For all
It is
Worth.

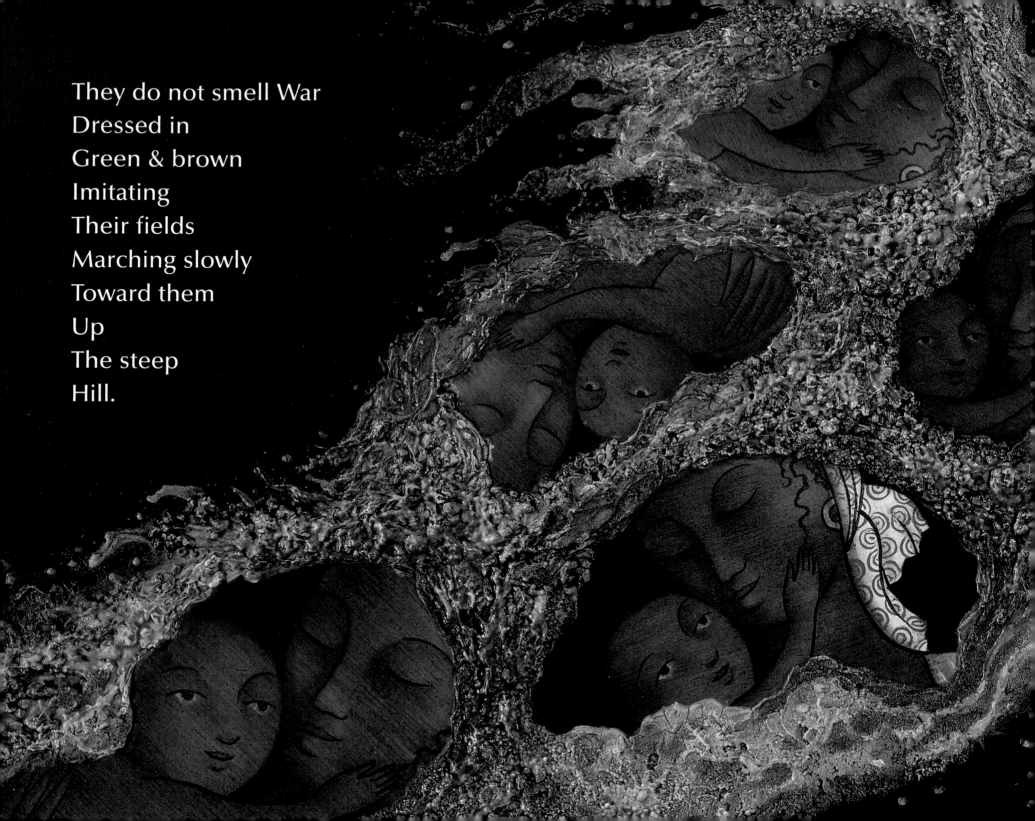

They do not smell War
Dressed in
Green & brown
Imitating
Their fields
Marching slowly
Toward them
Up
The steep
Hill.

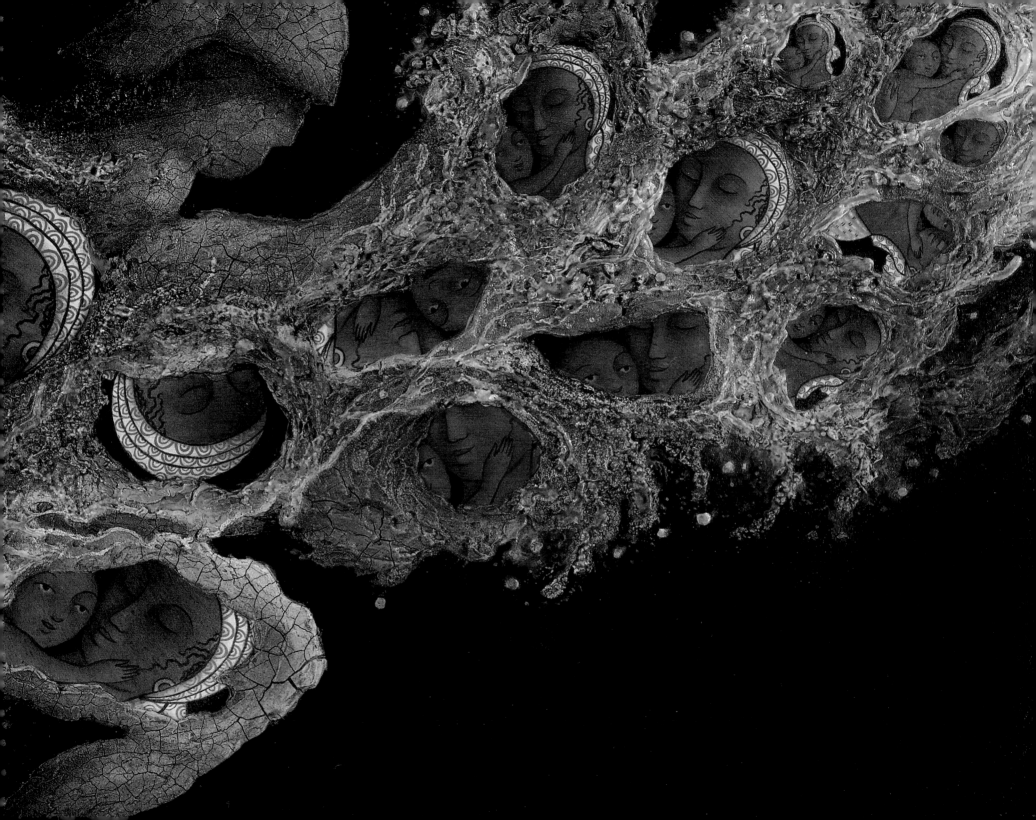

Though War is Old
It has not
Become wise
It will not hesitate
To destroy
Things that
Do not
Belong to it
Things very
Much older
Than itself.

Picture the forest
With its
Rivers
& rocks
Its pumas
&
Its
Parakeets
Its turtles
Leopards
&
Snakes.

High above them War
Has turned itself
Into a white cloud
Trailing
An
Airplane
That
Dusts
Everything
Below
With
A powder
That
Kills.

War has bad manners
War eats everything
In its path
& what
It doesn't
Eat
It
Dribbles
On:

Here
War is
Munching on
A village
Its missiles
Taking chunks
Big bites out
Of it.

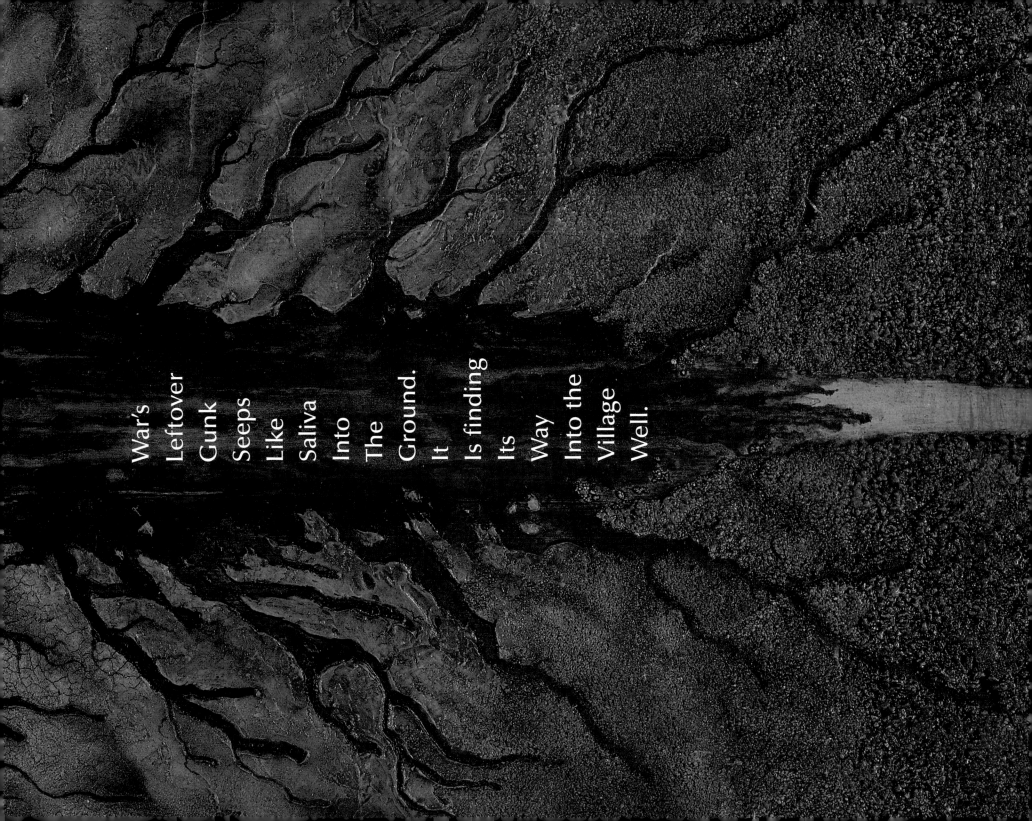

War's
Leftover
Gunk
Seeps
Like
Saliva
Into
The
Ground.
It
Is finding
Its
Way
Into the
Village
Well.

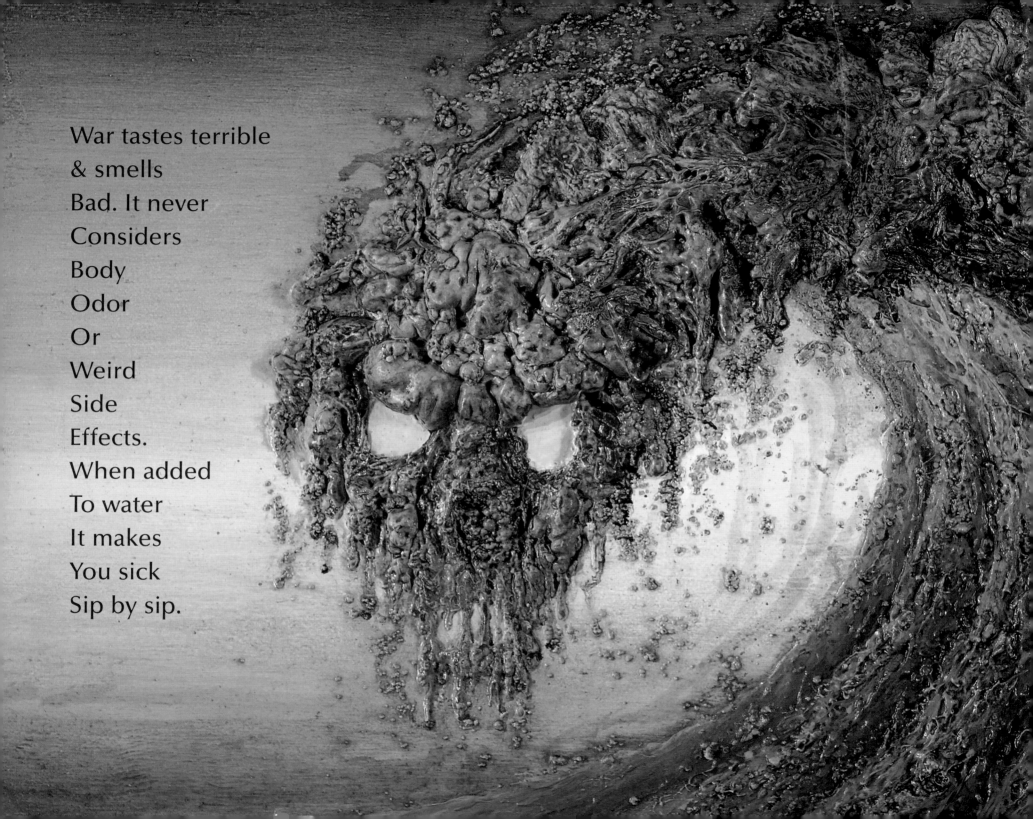

War tastes terrible
& smells
Bad. It never
Considers
Body
Odor
Or
Weird
Side
Effects.
When added
To water
It makes
You sick
Sip by sip.

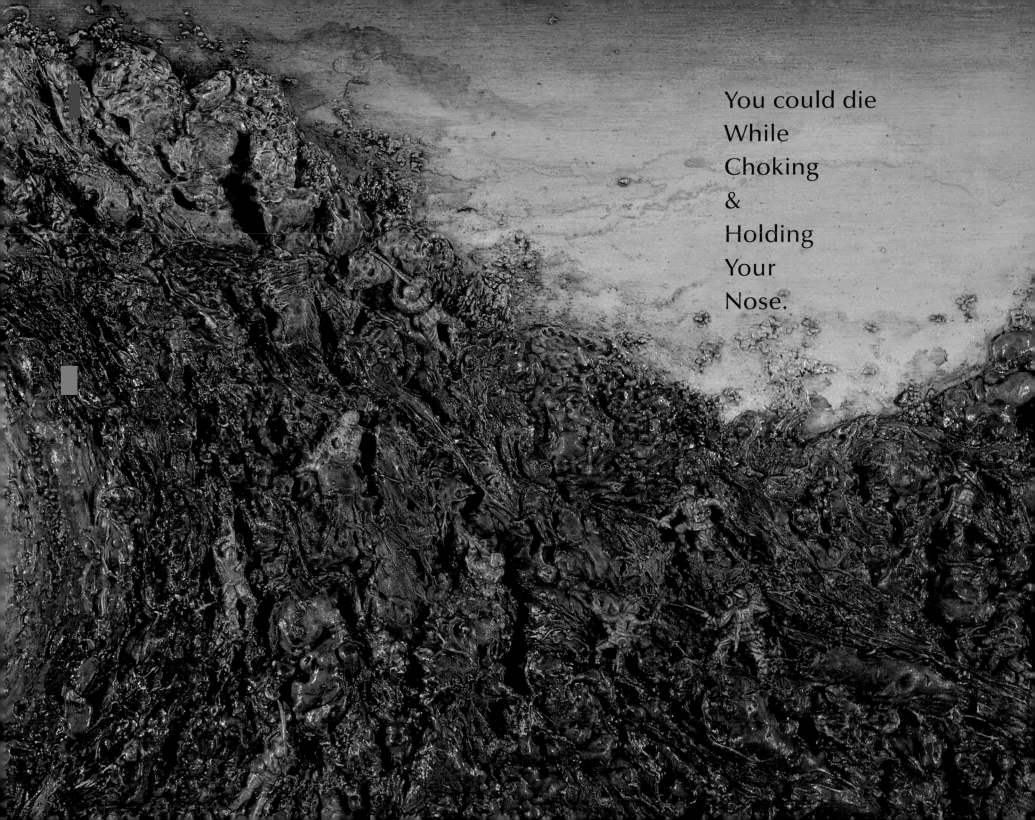

You could die
While
Choking
&
Holding
Your
Nose.

Now, suppose You
Become War
It happens
To some of
The nicest
People
On earth:
& one day
You have
To drink
The
Water
In this place.

To my global grandchildren
—A.W.

To Carlo, Federico, and Giacomo
—S.V.

Why War Is Never a Good Idea
Text copyright © 2007 by Alice Walker
Illustrations copyright © 2007 by Stefano Vitale
Manufactured in China.

Library of Congress Cataloging-in-Publication Data
Walker, Alice, date.
   Why war is never a good idea / Alice Walker ; illustrations by Stefano Vitale. —
1st ed.
      p.   cm.
   Summary: Simple, rhythmic text explores the wanton destructiveness of
War, which has grown old but not wise, as it demolishes nice people and
beautiful things with no consideration for the consequences.
   ISBN-13: 978-0-06-075385-6 (trade bdg.)
   ISBN-10: 0-06-075385-4 (trade bdg.)
   ISBN-13: 978-0-06-075386-3 (lib. bdg.)
   ISBN-10: 0-06-075386-2 (lib. bdg.)
   [1. War—Fiction.] I. Vitale, Stefano, ill. II. Title.
PZ7.W15213Why 2007   2006036255
[E]—dc22   CIP
                                                  AC

Design by Martha Rago
1 2 3 4 5 6 7 8 9 10 ❖ First Edition